We Celebrate the Eucharist

RuBEN

This program also includes
a Catechist's Guide,
Family Guide,
Program Director's Manual,
Celebrations Book, Posters,
and Record.

We Celebrate the Eucharist

Christiane Brusselmans

Brian A. Haggerty

SILVER BURDETT & GINN
MORRISTOWN, NJ

ACKNOWLEDGMENTS

Excerpts from *The New American Bible With Revised New Testament,* Copyright © 1986 by the Confraternity of Christian Doctrine, Washington, D.C., are used with permission. All rights reserved.

Excerpts from the English translation of *The Roman Missal* © 1985, International Committee on English in the Liturgy, Inc. All rights reserved.

Excerpts from the English translation of *Eucharistic Prayers for Masses with Children and for Masses of Reconciliation.* Copyright © 1975, International Committee on English in the Liturgy, Inc. All rights reserved.

Credits

viii: Andy Snow. 2: t. Silver Burdett; b. Treehaus Communications, Inc./Pottebaum. 10: b.l. Treehaus Communications, Inc./Pottebaum; b.r. Treehaus Communications, Inc./Pottebaum; t.r. Eugene Luttenberg/Art Resource. 18: b.l. Silver Burdett; b.r. Treehaus Communications, Inc./Pottebaum; t.r. Treehaus Communications, Inc./Pottebaum. 26: b.l. Andy Snow; c. Tony Freeman/Photo Edit; t.r. Jeffrey Reed/The Stock Shop. 34: l. Treehaus Communications, Inc./Pottebaum; t.r. Treehaus Communications, Inc./Pottebaum; b.r. Burk Uzzle/ Magnum. 42: t.l. H. Armstrong Roberts; t.r. Treehaus Communications, Inc./Pottebaum; b. Treehaus Communications, Inc./Pottebaum. 50: l. Tom Meyers; t.r. Charles Tucker/Taurus Photos; b.r. Treehaus Communications, Inc./Pottebaum. 58: t.l. Treehaus Communications, Inc./Pottebaum; t.r. Treehaus Communications, Inc./Pottebaum; b. Treehaus Communications, Inc./Pottebaum. 66: l. Hiroji Kubota/Magnum; t.r. Andy Snow; b.r. Harald Sund. 76: Silver Burdett.

Artist: Monique Piret Weyers

Hardcover edition   ISBN 0-382-00629-1
Softcover edition   ISBN 0-382-00628-3

Nihil Obstat
Reverend Anselm Murray, O.S.B
Censor Librorum

Imprimatur
✛ Most Reverend Frank J. Rodimer
Bishop of Paterson
January 3, 1989

The *nihil obstat* and *imprimatur* are official declarations that a book or pamphlet is free of doctrinal and moral error. No implication is contained therein that those who granted the *nihil obstat* and *imprimatur* agree with the contents, opinions, or statements expressed.

The contents and approach of the We Celebrate the Eucharist program are in accord with *Basic Teachings for Catholic Religious Education* issued by the National Conference of Catholic Bishops, the *General Catechetical Directory* issued by the Sacred Congregation for the Clergy, and *Sharing the Light of Faith, National Catechetical Directory for Catholics of the United States* issued by the United States Catholic Conference.

CONTENTS

Dear Family,
Your child's first reception
of the Eucharist can be one of the most
memorable experiences you will share with him or her.
This "golden book" represents a special invitation to you to help
support and guide your child on this unique journey.

You are not alone on your journey. We invite you to join with other families, catechists,
priests, and parish members in this privileged task. Because of the love you
have for your child, we ask you to participate, as only
you can, in this sacramental preparation.

This book belongs to your child. It is truly a "golden book." You and your child will discover
beautiful pictures, stories of Jesus from the Bible, and prayers that you can share with
all God's family when you join them in church to celebrate the Eucharist.
You will find pages on which your child's personal stories
can be drawn or written.
Great care will be invested in these pages. The fruit of this experience will be
offered to Jesus on your child's First Communion Day.
This book will be a keepsake of all you and your
child have experienced.

We wish you God's joy and peace as you
begin your journey to the table
of the Lord!

Christiane Brusselmans Brian A. Haggerty

1 The Eucharist Is About Belonging

How Good It Is to Belong to a Family

My name is Ruben

_____

The name of my family is

Romero

At home, there are people who love me.

I love them, too.
Their names are

mom
Dad
mozelle
Alexa

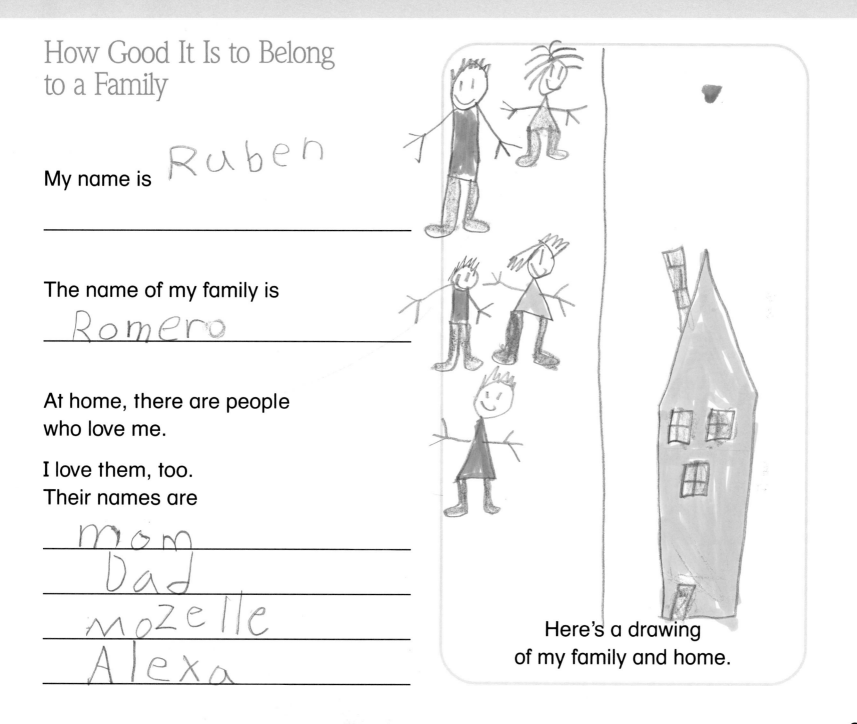

Here's a drawing
of my family and home.

3

God Calls Samuel

A long time ago, there lived a priest named Eli. He was very old and was going blind. A young boy named Samuel looked after him and was ministering with him in the temple. Samuel kept the light in the temple burning.

One night when Samuel was about to lie down to rest, the Lord called his name, "Samuel! Samuel!" So Samuel got up. He went to Eli and said, "Here I am. You called me."

Eli replied, "I did not call you. Go back to sleep." So Samuel went back and lay down again. But it happened that the Lord called him again, "Samuel! Samuel!" Samuel went back to Eli. He said, "Here I am. You called me."

Eli replied, "I did not call you. Go back to sleep." Samuel did not know the Lord yet. He did not know it was God calling him. For a third time the Lord called, "Samuel! Samuel!" Again he went to Eli and said, "Here I am. You called me."

Eli then understood that it was God who was calling Samuel. He told Samuel, "Go back and lie down. If someone calls you again, answer, 'Here I am, Lord. I am listening.' "

So Samuel went back to the temple. He lay down again to sleep. Then God called his name, "Samuel! Samuel!" Samuel answered, "Here I am, Lord. I am listening."

Samuel grew up and the Lord was with him. God stayed very close to Samuel. God made Samuel a great leader of his people.

Based on 1 Samuel 3:1–11

Here I am, Lord. Speak, Lord!
I am listening to your call.

Based on 1 Samuel 3:10

5

Belonging

When I was a baby,
my mother and father
wanted me to belong to
the Christian family.

They wanted me to become
a Christian.

They brought me to church
to be baptized.

The priest welcomed me
into God's house.

He asked my parents,
"What name do you give
your child?"

They answered,

Ruben

Then the priest asked
my parents,

"What do you ask of this
Christian community?"

They answered,

my child
to grow in fai-

The priest asked them,
"Will you help your child
grow in the faith?"

"Will you help your child
love God and neighbor
as Jesus showed us?"

My parents answered,
"Yes, we will."

Then I was baptized.

I will rejoice and be glad
each time I enter God's house.

Happy Are Those Who Belong to God's Family

God knows me by my name
and loves me.

As a mother and father
care for their child,
God cares for me.

I am very special. I belong to
the Christian family.

God says,
I have called you by your name,
and you are mine.

Based on Isaiah 43:1

God has chosen you as beloved
children. Therefore love one
another. Be always united. For you
are called to become one people.
Let the peace of Christ live in your
hearts. Always be thankful.

Based on Colossians 3:12–15

God's love is a special gift.
It is not meant to be kept
only for ourselves.

Love is a gift to be shared,
and given to others.

Here are some ways I can share
God's love with others.

Share my toys
Share my food

_____

_____

_____

_____

8

This is a picture of what I see when someone is baptized.

2 The Eucharist Is About
Celebrating

Happy Are Those Who Love to Celebrate Life

My family loves to have celebrations on special days.

On those days we invite special people to our home.

On my birthday I would like to invite

grandma

grandpa

Godmother

God gives us a special day every week to celebrate.

It is called

sunday mass

This is my drawing of a celebration I liked.

Jesus Is Invited to a Wedding

One day there was a wedding celebration in a town called Cana. Mary, the mother of Jesus, was there. Jesus was also there with some of his friends.

When there was no wine left for the rest of the celebration, Mary, the mother of Jesus, went to him and said, "Son, they have no more wine." Jesus answered, "Please, do not ask me to do anything about it now. My hour has not come yet." But Mary said to those serving, "Do whatever he tells you."

There were six very large stone water jars nearby. Jesus said to those who were serving, "Fill the jars with water." They filled them to the brim. Jesus told them, "Pour some out now and take it to the headwaiter."

The headwaiter tasted the water that had now become wine. He had no idea where the wine had come from. He then called the bridegroom and said, "Most people serve the best wine first. They save the cheaper wine until the guests have been drinking awhile. You have saved the best wine until the end of the celebration."

This is the first wonderful sign that Jesus gave to his friends. His friends began to believe in him.

When the celebration was over, Jesus, his mother, and his friends went down to Capernaum and stayed there for a few days.

Based on John 2:1–11

I rejoiced when I heard them say, "Let us go to God's house."

Based on Psalm 121:1

13

We Come Together as a Community

There is a special house
in my neighborhood.

We call it a church.

Many men, women, and
children gather there on Sunday
to celebrate the Lord's Day.

They greet one another.
They pray and sing to
the Lord Jesus.

Jesus says,
Where two or three come together
in my name, I am there with them.

Based on Matthew 18:20

Glory to God in the highest,
and peace to his people on earth.

Lord God, heavenly King,
almighty God and Father,
  we worship you,
  we give you thanks,
  we praise you for your glory.

Lord Jesus Christ,
only Son of the Father,
Lord God, Lamb of God,
you take away the sin
of the world:
  have mercy on us;
you are seated at the right hand
of the Father: receive our prayer.

For you alone are the Holy One,
you alone are the Lord,
you alone are the Most High,
  Jesus Christ,
  with the Holy Spirit,
  in the glory of God the Father.
Amen.

15

Happy Are Those Who Celebrate the Lord's Day

Every week Jesus invites us
to come to a celebration
in God's house.

We are Jesus'
sisters and brothers.
We gather together
as one family.

We come together
to worship God
who is always with us.

This is the day of the Lord.
Rejoice and be glad
when they say to you,
Let us go to God's house!

Based on Psalm 122:1

Here are the names
of some of the people who
join me on Sunday to celebrate
the Lord's Day.

mom

dad

mozzle

Alexa

16

Here I am with my family in God's house.

3 The Eucharist Is About Listening

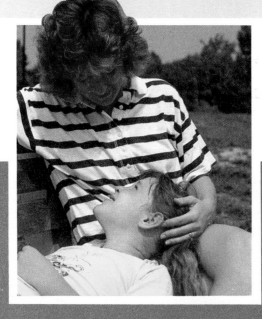

Happy Are Those Who Listen Well

These are some voices
I like to listen to.

birds

~~wind~~ ducks

These are some sounds
I like to hear.

wind

the ocean,

Priest

father

jerry

Here is someone I like to listen to.

Mary Listens to Jesus

One day, Jesus was on a journey. He came to a village where two sisters, Martha and Mary, lived.

Martha welcomed Jesus into their home. Her sister, Mary, sat down with Jesus and listened to all he was saying. Martha, instead, was very busy with all the work that had to be done.

Martha said to Jesus, "Lord, do you not care that my sister is leaving me to do all the serving myself? Please tell her to help me."

Jesus answered, "Martha, Martha, you worry about so many things. They are important. But the most important thing is to be with me and to listen to my words. Mary has chosen to listen to my words. That shall not be taken away from her."

Based on Luke 10:38–42

Lord, open my ears and my heart to your words.

Based on Acts 16:14

21

The Bible

The Bible teaches us the story of God's people.

At the Eucharist we listen carefully to words from the Bible.

In the Old Testament, the prophets tell us how God loves us and promises to send a savior.

To respond to this message of love, we often sing a psalm.

In the New Testament, the first Christians tell us how to live the teachings of Jesus.

The gospel teaches us about Jesus, God's Son.

Jesus lives with us. He shows us how much God loves us. This is the "good news."

To welcome the good news, we stand and sing:

Alleluia, Alleluia, Alleluia!

Happy are those who hear the word of God.

Jesus says,
If you hear the word of God and live by it, you are my friends and true members of my family.

Based on Luke 8:21

23

Happy Are Those Who Listen to God's Word

John, a good friend of Jesus, calls Jesus the Word of God.

Jesus also gives us other ways to name him.

He tells us:

I am the bread of life.

I am the light of the world.

I am the good shepherd.

I am the resurrection and the life.

I am the way, and the truth, and the life.

I am the true vine.

Based on the Gospel According to John

Here are some of my favorite words of Jesus.

life

joy

pray

peace

euchirist

love

faith

share

happy

truth

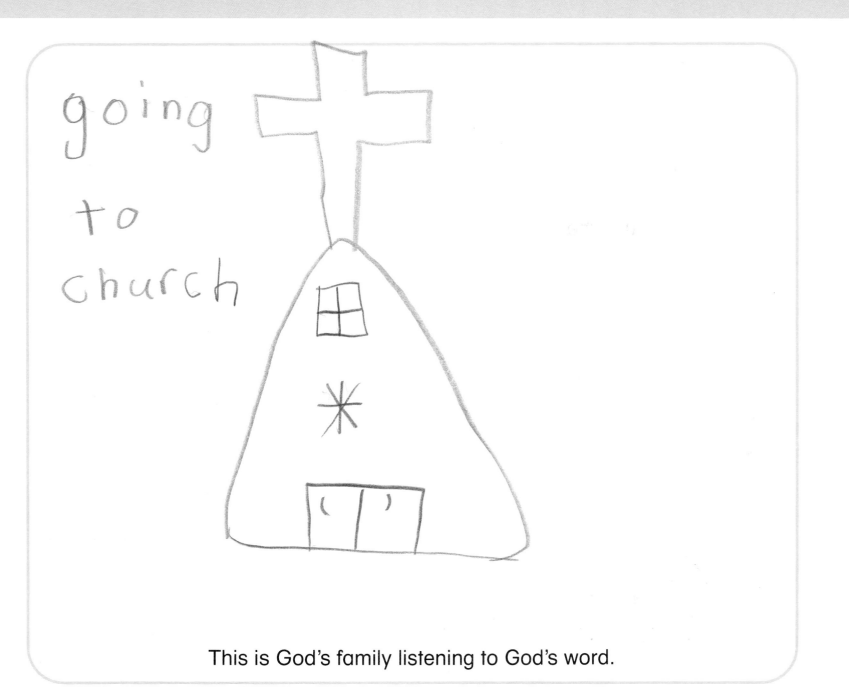

going to church

This is God's family listening to God's word.

4 The Eucharist Is About Caring

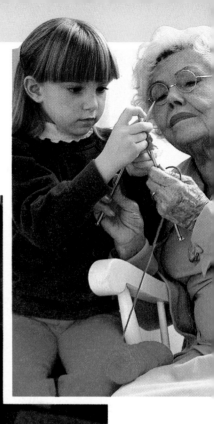

Happy Are Those Who Care for People

Many people care for me
at home, at school,
and in my neighborhood.

I care for people, too.

Here are some things I do
to show I care.

When someone feels lonely,

I play with them.

When someone feels sad,

I cheer them up.

When someone is sick,

I take care of
them.

When someone is left out,

I also play

with them.

POOR

Here are some people
who need love and care.

Jesus Cares for a Paralyzed Man

When Jesus returned to Capernaum, word went around that he was back home. Many people came to the house where Jesus was staying to hear him speak. The house was very crowded. There was no room left, even in front of the door.

While Jesus was teaching, four men arrived carrying a man on a stretcher. The man on the stretcher was paralyzed and could not walk. His friends wanted him to meet Jesus. They could not get in through the door because of the crowd, so they climbed up onto the roof. They made an opening in the roof and lowered the stretcher into the house.

Jesus saw how much they had trusted and believed in him. He said to the paralyzed man, "My friend, your sins are forgiven."

Some of the people who were sitting there had a hard time understanding that Jesus could forgive sins. They believed that only God can forgive sins.

Jesus knew what they were thinking. He said to them, "If I can heal this man and make him walk again, will you believe that I can forgive sins as well?" Then Jesus said to the man, "Stand up, my friend. Pick up your stretcher and go home." The man got up at once, picked up his stretcher, and walked out in front of everyone.

Everyone who was there saw what had happened and praised God. They said, "We have never seen anything like this."

Based on Mark 2:1–12

Happy are those who help the poor and the sick. The Lord will give them life and make them happy.

Based on Psalm 41:2–3

Prayer of the Faithful

In God's family we pray
for one another at the
celebration of the Eucharist.

We call this prayer the
Prayer of the Faithful.

Here is one way we can say
this prayer.

For God's family all over the world,
Lord, hear our prayer.

For the leaders of God's family,
Lord, hear our prayer.

For the leaders of our country,
Lord, hear our prayer.

For our parents and teachers,
Lord, hear our prayer.

For our friends and neighbors,
Lord, hear our prayer.

For those who have no work,
Lord, hear our prayer.

For those who have no homes,
Lord, hear our prayer.

For those who have no food,
Lord, hear our prayer.

For those who are sick,
Lord, hear our prayer.

For those who are alone,
Lord, hear our prayer.

For those who are in prison,
Lord, hear our prayer.

For those who suffer from war,
Lord, hear our prayer.

Happy Are Those Who Open Their Hearts to People in Need

Jesus says,

Happy are those who
share with others.

Happy are those who
comfort others.

Happy are those who
are gentle and kind.

Happy are those who
treat others fairly.

Happy are those who
forgive others.

Happy are those who
love God.

Happy are those who
make peace.

Happy are those
who are faithful.

Based on Matthew 5:3–11

I know people who try
to put these words of Jesus
into practice.

Here are their names
and what they do.

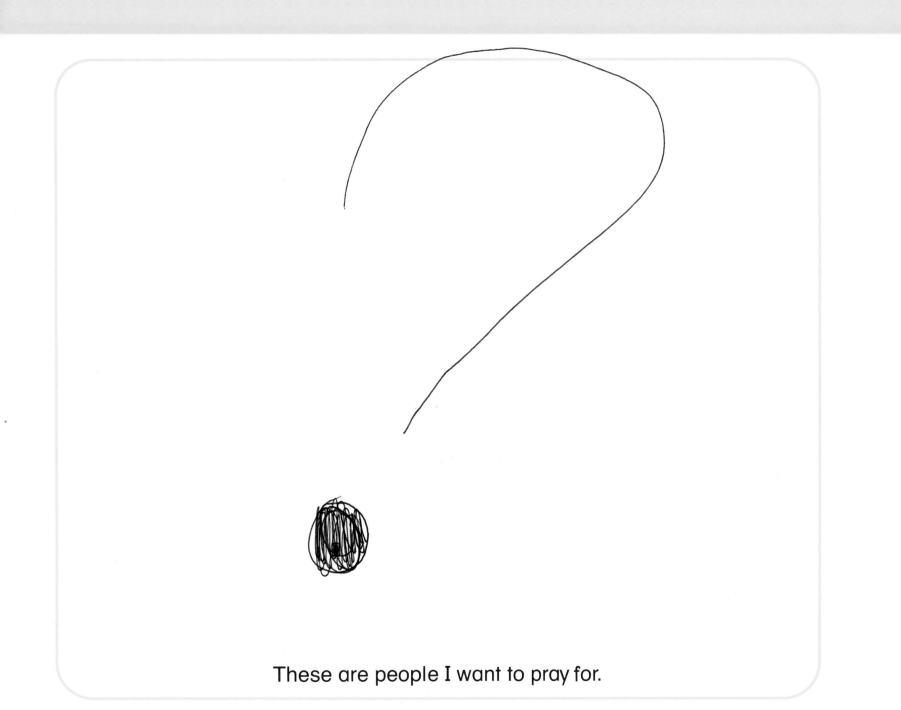

These are people I want to pray for.

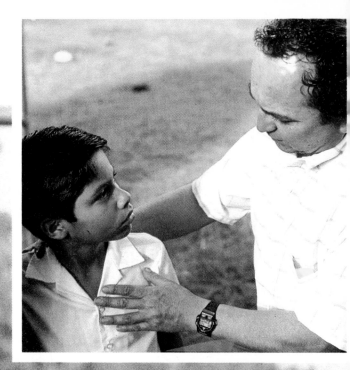

Happy Are Those Who Make Peace

It is often hard to share,
to play with everybody,
to forgive, and to
make peace.

Sometimes I do not get along
with my parents,
my brothers and sisters,
or my friends.

What can I do about it?

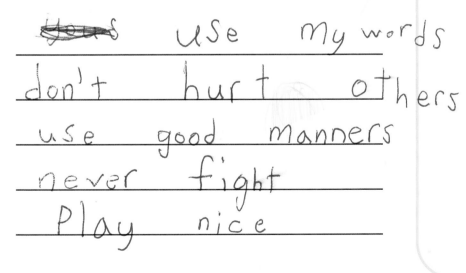

use my words
don't hurt others
use good manners
never fight
Play nice

Here I am making up
after a quarrel.

35

Father and Son Make Peace

One day Jesus told this story. There was a man who had two sons. The younger son said to his father, "Let me have my share of our property now." So the father divided the property between his two sons.

A few days later the younger son packed all he had and left home. He went to a faraway country and wasted all his money. There was a famine in that country and he became hungry and cold.

A local farmer hired him to feed pigs. The young man was so hungry that he would gladly have eaten the husks the pigs ate. But no one offered him anything.

When he came to his senses, he said to himself, "The people who work for my father have more than enough food, and here I am starving to death. I am going back home. I will tell my father how sorry I am." So he started home.

While he was still a long way off, his father saw him coming. The father ran out to meet his son. He took him in his arms and kissed him.

The young son began to say, "Father, I have sinned against heaven and you. I am no longer worthy to be called your son." But his father said to his servants, "Quick! Bring out the best clothing and sandals. Prepare a meal. Let us celebrate! My son was dead and has come back to life. He was lost and has been found." And they began the celebration.

Based on Luke 15:11–24

Lord, give me joy when I come back to you.

Based on Psalm 51:14–15

Lord, Give Us Your Peace

In God's family we ask for
God's forgiveness and
peace in many ways.

At the celebration of the
Eucharist we say,

Lord, have mercy.
Christ, have mercy.
Lord, have mercy.

We give one another
the sign of peace.

The peace of the Lord
be with you always.

With John the Baptist,
we say,

Lamb of God, you take away
the sins of the world:
have mercy on us.

Jesus teaches us how to pray:

Our Father,
who art in heaven,
hallowed be thy name;

thy kingdom come;
thy will be done on earth
as it is in heaven.

Give us this day
our daily bread;
and forgive us our trespasses
as we forgive those
who trespass against us;

and lead us not
into temptation,
but deliver us from evil.

For the kingdom, the power
and the glory are yours,
now and forever.

Amen.

Based on Matthew 6: 9–13

Happy Are Those Who Ask Forgiveness and Make Peace

The Spirit of Jesus
lives in my heart
and helps me to know
how to please God,
and how to make
others happy.

The Spirit of peace
helps me to see
when I have hurt
someone.

The Spirit of love
helps me to love and forgive
those who have hurt me.

Saint Paul says:
Because you are
God's chosen ones,
let your hearts be full
of gentleness and kindness.

Forgive one another
as the Lord forgives you.

May the peace
that Jesus gives
live in your hearts.

Based on Colossians 3:12–15

Preist

Here are people sharing the sign of peace at Mass.

6 The Eucharist Is About Giving Thanks for Creation

Happy Are Those Who Give Thanks for Creation

Praise to you, Lord,
for our brother the sun,
beautiful and radiant;
by him you give us light.

For our brother the wind, for the air,
and the clouds, for the clear sky,
and for every kind of weather.

For our sister, the water.
She is so useful,
so precious, and so pure.

For our brother the fire,
who makes us warm;
by him you light up the night.

For our mother the earth,
who carries us and feeds us.
She gives us her plants
and her colorful fruits.

Praise to you, Lord, for all creatures!

from Saint Francis

food

Here are some of
God's gifts to me.

The Poem of Creation

In the beginning, God created the heavens and the earth.

God said, "Let there be light!" And there was light. God called the light "day" and the darkness "night." Evening and morning came. And God saw that it was good.

Then God said, "Let there be dry land and water around the land!" God called the dry land "earth" and the water "sea." Evening and morning came. And God saw that it was good.

Then God said, "Let the earth produce plants and trees that bear all kinds of fruit!" And so it was. Evening and morning came. And God saw that it was good.

Then God said, "Let there be a great light to shine over the day, and let there be smaller lights to shine during the night!" God called the greater light "sun." The smaller lights God called "moon" and "stars." Evening and morning came. And God saw that it was good.

Then God said, "Let the waters be filled with all kinds of fish. Let the sky be filled with all kinds of birds. Let the earth be filled with all kinds of animals!" Evening and morning came. God saw that it was good.

Then God said, "Let us make men and women in our own image!" So people were created to share God's own life. God blessed them and said, "Take care of all that I have created. It is yours." God looked at everything and saw that it was very good. Evening and morning came. God saw that it was good.

Based on Genesis 1:1–31

The Lord has done wonderful things for me. Holy is God's name.

Based on Luke 1:49

45

The Thanksgiving Prayer

The Lord be with you.

And also with you.

Lift up your hearts.

We lift them up to the Lord.

Let us give thanks
to the Lord our God.

It is right to give him
thanks and praise.

God our father,
you have brought us here together
so that we can give you
    thanks and praise
for all the wonderful things
    you have done.

We thank you for all that is
    beautiful in the world
and for all the happiness
    you have given us.

We know that you are good.
You love us and do
    great things for us.
So we all sing together.

Holy, holy, holy Lord,
    God of power and might.
Heaven and earth are full
    of your glory.
        Hosanna in the highest.

Blessed is he who comes
    in the name of the Lord.
        Hosanna in the highest.

God, you love us very much.
Because of this great love,
you sent Jesus to save us.

If we open our hearts
to his light and his love,
Jesus will give us
a new life and make us
children of God.

Happy Are Those Who Give Thanks to the Lord

This is my prayer
to thank God for sending
us Jesus.

thank you for the for ~~the~~

world so sweet thank

for the food

we eat thank

you for birds

that ~~thing~~ sing

thank god

for everything.

thank you god for cars.

This is my drawing to thank God
for all God's gifts.

GOD'S LOVE GIVES US JESUS

Here is how I decorate this page.

7 The Eucharist Is About Giving Thanks for New Life

Happy Are Those Who Share Their Life and Love

Day after day, parents love their children.

They spend their lives and time for them.

This is what my parents do for me.

give me food
they give me clothes.
they give me time

I, too, can share my love and my life with others in many ways.

Here are some of them.

do not be mad.

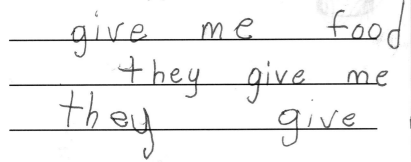

Here are people who share their life and love with others.

Jesus Lives a New Life

Early on Sunday morning, Mary Magdalene went to the tomb where Jesus' body had been buried. She saw that the stone had been rolled away from the entrance to the tomb.

Mary stood by the tomb crying. Looking into the tomb she saw two angels sitting in the place where Jesus' body had been. The angels asked Mary, "Why are you crying?" She answered, "Because someone has taken my Lord away, and I don't know where to find him."

Then Mary turned around. She saw Jesus standing there, but she did not recognize him. Jesus said to her, "Why are you crying?" Thinking he was the gardener,

Mary said to him, "If you have taken him away, tell me where you have laid him and I will go and find him."

Jesus said, "Mary!" Now Mary knew that this was Jesus. She said to him, "Rabbouni!" which means teacher. Jesus said to her, "Go to my friends and tell them, 'I am returning to my Father and to your Father, to my God and your God.' "

Mary went to the disciples and said, "I have seen the Lord!" And she told them all that Jesus had said to her.

Based on John 20:11–18

The Lord is truly risen.
Alleluia! Alleluia! Alleluia!

Based on Luke 24:34

53

We Remember

At every Eucharist we do what
Jesus did with his friends the
night before he died.

During a meal, Jesus took
bread. He gave thanks
and praise. He broke the bread,
gave it to his friends, and said:

Take this, all of you,
and eat it,
for this is my body.
This is my life,
which is given for you.

Then Jesus took a cup of wine.
He gave thanks and praise.

He blessed the cup, gave it to
his friends, and said:

Take this, all of you,
and drink from it,
for this is my blood.
This is my life,
which is poured out for you.

Do this in memory of me.

Adapted from the
Eucharistic Prayer
for Children

Happy Are Those Who Share in the New Life of Jesus

We proclaim our faith.

When we eat this bread and drink
this cup, we proclaim your death,
Lord Jesus, until you come in glory.

Lord, because you love us,
you invite us to come
to your table.

Jesus says,
There is no greater love than to
give your life for your friends.

Based on John 15:13

Jesus gives his life for us.
This is his sacrifice.

The Bible tells us:
Do not forget to do good deeds.
Share what you have. These are
the sacrifices that please God.

Based on Hebrews 13:16

Give your life for one another.
In this way you share in the
sacrifice of Jesus.

Jesus died for us.

Here is how Jesus shares his life and love with us.

8 The Eucharist Is About Sharing a Meal

Happy Are Those Who Share a Meal

We thank God
for the food we have
and for the Spirit of joy
and love we share.

When we share a meal
with others, we share our
life and love with them.

My parents work
many hours to
buy the food we need.

They share their time
and talent to prepare the food
for the table. I help in
whatever way I can.

When everything is ready,
we sit at the table. We thank God
for the food we share
and enjoy our meal together.

when we got
our house
blesed the
preist ate
with us.

priest me
dad mom
alexa
mozzle

Here's my family
eating a special meal.

Jesus Shares a Meal with Friends

Two of Jesus' friends were walking to the village of Emmaus. They were talking about Jesus.

Jesus himself joined them on their journey. Somehow, the two men did not recognize him. Jesus asked, "Why do you look so sad? What are you talking about?" One of them answered Jesus, "Haven't you heard about Jesus of Nazareth? He was a great prophet. Everyone saw his great power and love. We thought Jesus was the one who would make us free, but our leaders had him crucified. He died three days ago. Now, this morning, some women in our group saw Jesus. They said he was risen from the dead."

Jesus said to them, "You just don't seem to believe what the prophets have been saying. It was necessary for the savior to suffer these things and to enter into glory."

It was almost evening when they reached Emmaus. The two disciples asked Jesus to stay with them for the evening meal. While Jesus was with them at table, he broke bread, blessed it, and gave it to them to eat. As Jesus did this, their eyes were opened and they recognized him.

When Jesus left, the disciples were so happy that they went to Jerusalem to tell the others what had happened. They told how they had recognized Jesus in the breaking of the bread.

Based on Luke 24:13–35

Stay with us, Lord Jesus. Be with us at all times.

Based on Luke 24:29

61

The Lord's Table

Jesus often
shared a meal with
his family and friends.

On the night before he died,
Jesus shared a special meal
with his friends and said,
"I have wanted so much
to eat this meal with you."

Today Jesus calls us to gather
around the Lord's table.

Happy are those who are called
to his supper.

When we see the bread of life
and the cup of blessing, we say,

Lord, I am not worthy to receive
you, but only say the word and I
shall be healed.

We receive the bread of life and
the cup of blessing with our families
and many of Jesus' friends.

The body of Christ.
Amen.

The blood of Christ.
Amen.

We sing joyfully as we gather around
the table of the Lord.

63

Happy Are Those Who Share in the Lord's Supper

I am now ready to share
in the supper of the Lord.

The bread I shall receive
is very special.
It is the bread of life.

Jesus says:
I am the bread of life. If you eat this
bread you will live forever. I will live
in you and you in me.

Based on John 6:51, 56

The bread that we break
is a sharing in the risen
body of Jesus.

The cup of blessing that we bless
is a sharing in the new
life of Jesus.

Based on I Corinthians 10:16

Jesus says:
Take this and share it. This cup,
which is poured out for you, is the
new covenant in my blood.

Based on Luke 22:17–22

When I receive the Eucharist,
I am one with the Lord,
one with my family, and
one with God's family.

This is how my family and I will celebrate
my First Holy Communion.

9 The Eucharist Is About Going Forth to Make a Better World

Happy Are Those Who Love and Help One Another

What does my family do for me?

Give me clothes

What do my teachers and classmates do for me?

they teach me things.

What do my neighbors and friends do for me?

Play with me.

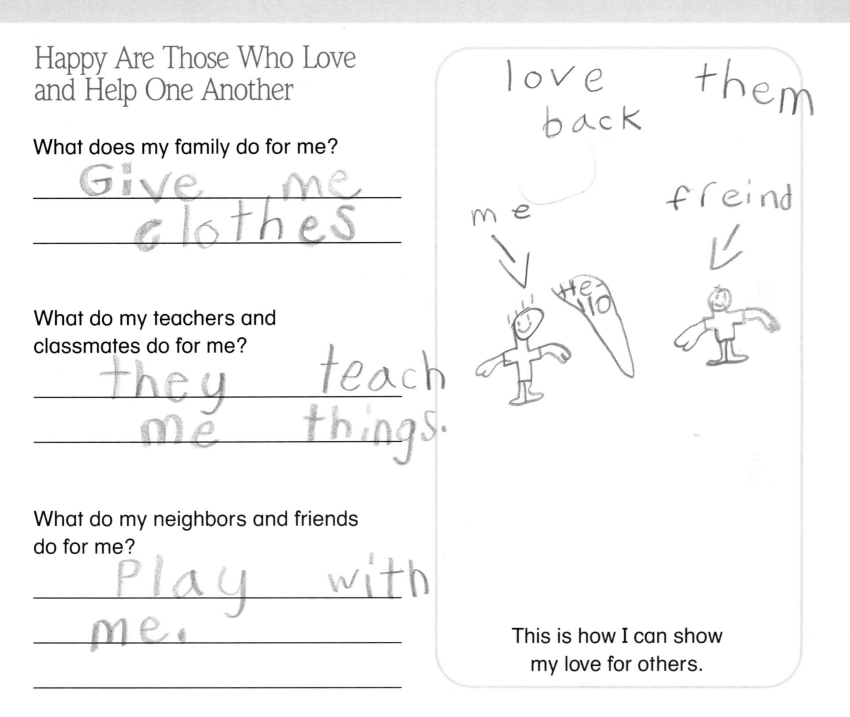

love them
back

me   freind

Hello

This is how I can show
my love for others.

God's Way to a Better World

One day, Jesus will come again. He will say to those who have lived as he taught:

"Come and receive your share in the kingdom I have prepared for you. I was hungry and you gave me food. I was thirsty and you gave me a drink. I was a stranger and you made me feel welcome. I had nothing to wear and you gave me clothes. I was sick and you took care of me. I was in prison and you visited me."

The people who hear these words will ask Jesus, "Lord, when did we do all these things?" Jesus will say to them: "As long as you did these things for one of my brothers and sisters, you did it for me. You have God's blessing. Come and live forever in the kingdom which has been prepared for you."

Based on Matthew 25:34–40

We shall be God's people.
God will be with us forever.

Based on Revelations 21:3

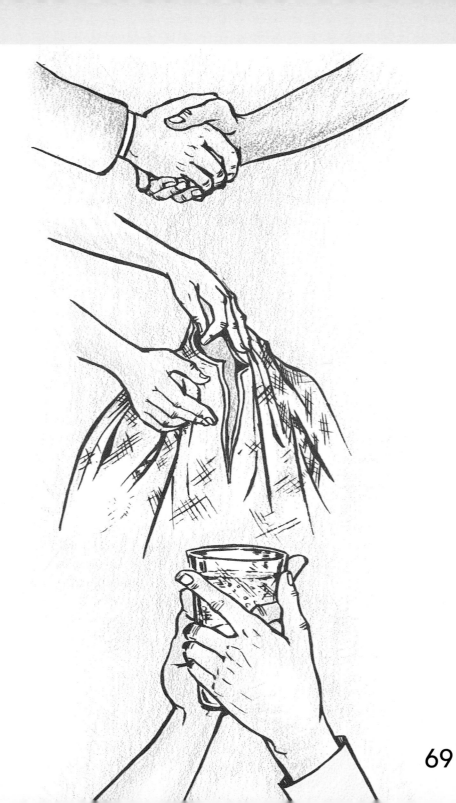

May Your Joy Fill the Earth

After we receive the
Eucharist, we all come
back to our seats.

We keep silent for a while.

The Spirit of Jesus
helps us think of good ideas
for bringing joy
and love to people.

Jesus says,
As I have been sent into the world,
now I am sending you.

Based on John 20:21

We receive a blessing.

May Almighty God bless you,
the Father, and the Son,
and the Holy Spirit.

We make the sign of the cross
and answer,

Amen.

We are sent forth.

Go in peace to love
and serve the Lord.

We answer,

Thanks be to God.

We leave
God's house
with a joyful song
and greet our friends.

John tells us of a holy city where
God will make all things new.

In this city there will be no more tears,
no more pain, no more death.

Let us go with joy
to the house of the Lord.
Based on Psalm 122:1

Jesus shall be with us forever.
Based on Revelation 21

Amen. Come, Lord Jesus!
Revelation 22:20

Happy are those who will enter this holy city.

A Review
Of What I Have Learned
To Help Me Grow
In God's Family

1. The Eucharist Is About Belonging

God knows me by my name and loves me.

I was welcomed into God's family on the day I was baptized.

2. The Eucharist Is About Celebrating

Whenever we gather as God's family, Jesus is present among us. Jesus says, "Where two or three come together in my name, I am there with them."

When we gather on Sunday as God's family, we celebrate the resurrection of Jesus.

3. The Eucharist Is About Listening

Jesus tells us how important it is to listen to his words. Jesus says, "If you listen to my words and live by them, you are my friends."

We listen to the words of Jesus when the Bible is read to us at Mass.

Prayer is the special name we use for talking and listening to God.

4. The Eucharist Is About Caring

We should pray for each other, especially for those people who need our love and care.

I can show love and care for my parents, my sisters and brothers, my friends and teachers, and other people who need me.

5. The Eucharist Is About Making Peace

We do not always get along with others, but we can always try to be better. We can ask God and others for forgiveness when we need it.

Jesus gives us his Spirit to help us to know how to love God. The Spirit helps us to know how to make others happy. The Spirit helps us to make peace.

6. The Eucharist Is About Giving Thanks for Creation

During the Eucharist we thank God for the gift of life, for Jesus, for our families and friends, and all the things we love and enjoy.

7. The Eucharist Is About Giving Thanks for New Life

Jesus wanted to stay with us forever, so on the night before he died, Jesus had supper with his best friends. At that supper, which we call the last supper, Jesus broke some bread and gave it to his friends. He said, "Take this and eat it. This is my body, which I am going to give for you. Do this in memory of me." Each time we receive the Eucharist, Jesus is with us in a special way.

8. The Eucharist Is About Sharing A Meal

Jesus tells us, "I am the bread of life. If you eat this bread, I will live in you and you in me."

9. The Eucharist Is About Going Forth to Make a Better World

After we leave Mass we bring the joy and love of God's Spirit to others.

When Jesus comes in glory, he will gather people from all over the world to be with him in happiness and peace forever.

On the _____17_____ day of _____April_____ ,

in the year of Our Lord _____ ,

in the Christian Community of _____ ,

located in

_____

_____
(child)

shared fully in the Eucharistic Celebration

by receiving Holy Communion.

_____   _____   _____
(parent)   (catechist)   (celebrant)

These people were present to celebrate my

First Communion Day with me.